SET YOUR HOUSE *in* ORDER

A Workbook to Organize Your Finances and Plan Your Estate

CROWN FINANCIAL MINISTRIES

CROWN.ORG

March 2005

INTRODUCTION

Many people realize that their financial affairs are not completely in order. The *Set Your House In Order* workbook is designed to enable you to assemble and organize your important financial information in one place.

You will need to secure a 3-ring binder (the spine should be a minimum of one inch) and **eight tab dividers**. The pages of *Set Your House In Order* have been perforated and 3-hole punched. Remove them from the workbook and place each section in the binder in consecutive order under the tab dividers.

Completing *Set Your House In Order* usually requires from one to two hours for each section. The amount of time will be determined by the complexity of your financial situation and the amount of planning and organization you have done in the past.

This workbook is designed to help you organize your finances and plan your estate. Those who do not leave their loved ones a well-organized estate do them a tremendous disservice. Settling a disorganized estate is usually more expensive, and it compounds the emotional stress survivors experience.

A Word about Crown Financial Ministries

The purpose of Crown Financial Ministries is teaching people God's financial principles in order to know Christ more intimately and to be free to serve Him.

IMPORTANT NOTICE!

This workbook is intended to serve as an aid in assembling your financial data. No decisions concerning insurance, investments, ownership of assets, estate planning and any legal documents should be made without the advice and assistance of competent professionals, including attorneys, accountants and financial planners.

T A B L E   O F   C O N T E N T S

Section	Subject	Forms
1	Personal Financial Statement / Document Organizer	Personal Financial Statement and Location of Important Documents
2	Estimated Monthly Budget / Future Income	Estimated Monthly Budget, Social Security, Company Retirement Benefits and Estimate of Future Income
3	Advisors / Safe-Deposit Box / Debt List / Accounts	List of Advisors, Safe-Deposit Box Inventory, Debt List, Bank Accounts, Credit Cards and Computer Instructions
4	Asset Inventory	Automobiles / Personal Property / Investments and Real Estate
5	Insurance	Insurance Inventory and Summary of Company Insurance
6	Estate Documents	Estate Documents Checklist, Distribution of Household Possessions and Funeral Instructions
7	Family / Optional Ideas	Personal History, Helpful Household Answers, Major Home Improvements, Items Loaned to Others, When Your Marital Status Changes, Incompetence or Disability, Remarriage and Memo to My Family

There are three assignments in this section: the Personal Financial Statement, the Document Organizer and the Location of Important Documents form.

I. Personal Financial Statement

The Personal Financial Statement helps you to get a picture of your current financial situation. Estimate the value of each asset and the amount of each liability. Bring the completed Personal Financial Statement with you to class if you are enrolled in the study.

> * We recommend that you revise your financial statement once a year to help you keep abreast of your financial progress. It is wise to complete an annual list of all your individual investments, noting their value.

II. Document Organizer

The primary purpose of the Document Organizer you will create is to gather all your important papers in one place and to organize them in a systematic way. This will be helpful as you complete the other sections of this workbook. If you discover you are missing any important document, make an effort to obtain it promptly.

Once you have determined how many documents you want to place in the Organizer, obtain an adequate number of file folders along with an accordion file folder or file cabinet in which to store them.

Some documents such as wills, trusts, deeds and life insurance policies should be stored in a secure place, such as a safe-deposit box. Photocopy the originals of these documents and place the copies in the Document Organizer.

You should consider placing some of the following items in the Document Organizer:

■ Birth Certificates	■ Deeds
■ Marriage Certificates	■ Mortgages
■ Military Discharges	■ Leases
■ Wills	■ Business Agreements
■ Trusts	■ Retirement Papers
■ Debt Instruments	■ Automobile Titles
■ Power of Attorney	■ Insurance Policies
■ Death Certificates	■ Divorce Decrees
■ Citizenship Papers	■ Income Tax Returns

III. Location of Important Documents

The third assignment for this section is to complete the Location of Important Documents form. This will allow you to find any item quickly. Complete this in pencil to allow for changes.

PERSONAL FINANCIAL STATEMENT

Date _____

ASSETS (present market value)

Cash on hand / checking account

Savings / money market

Stocks / bonds / mutual funds

Cash value of life insurance

Coins

Home

Other real estate

Mortgages / notes receivable

Business valuation

Automobiles / other vehicles

Furniture

Jewelry

Other personal property

IRA / 401 K

Pension / retirement plan

Other Assets

TOTAL ASSETS:

LIABILITIES (Current amount owed)

Credit card debt

Automobile loans

Home mortgage

Other real estate mortgages

Personal debts to relatives

Business loans

Educational loans

Medical / Other past due bills

Life insurance loans

Bank loans

Other debts and loans

TOTAL LIABILITIES:

NET WORTH   (total assets minus total liabilities):

9

LOCATION OF IMPORTANT DOCUMENTS

Date _____

Documents	Location of Original	Location of Copy
Birth Certificates		
Marriage Certificate		
Military Discharge		
Wills		
Trusts		
Debt Instruments		
Power of Attorney		
Death Certificates		
Citizenship Papers		
Divorce Decree		
Deeds		
Leases		
Business Agreements		
Retirement Papers		
Automobile Titles		
Insurance Policies		
Income Tax Files		
Social Security Card		
Other Documents		

In this section you will complete your Estimated Budget and will estimate your future income.

I. Estimated Budget

The Estimated Budget is designed to give you a picture of your current income and spending. This is an especially important exercise, and for many people it proves to be difficult. You may not know what you are spending. You may be frustrated by what your Estimated Monthly Budget reveals. You may need to reduce spending to balance your budget. *But be encouraged* — recognizing the financial facts will put you in a position to make wise, informed decisions.

If you are married, work on this together with your spouse to foster good communication. Complete the following steps:

1. List Monthly Gross Income

List all income (before taxes) in the "Gross Monthly Income" section on page 25. When all or part of your income consists of commissions or other fluctuating sources, average it for a year and divide by twelve to compute your monthly income. Business expense reimbursements should not be considered income.

2. Subtract Giving and Taxes

Deduct your monthly giving and income taxes (Federal withholding, social security and state and local taxes) from gross income to determine Net Spendable Income.

Payroll deductions for insurance, retirement, union dues, etc. **should not** be subtracted from your gross income. Include them in spendable income and deduct them from the proper category so that you will have a more accurate picture of your spending. For example, if a payroll deduction is made for health insurance, this amount should be considered as a part of income and as an expense under the Insurance Category.

3. Determine How Net Spendable Income is Spent

Net Spendable Income (your living expenses) is divided into eleven categories. List how much you spend in each category.

4. Compute the Surplus or Deficit

Insert the Net Spendable Income. Then add the expenses under each of the eleven categories and note this on the Total Living Expenses line. Subtract Total Living Expenses from Net Spendable Income to determine whether you have a surplus or deficit in your budget each month.

II. Future Estimated Income

Estimate your future income to determine how much you are scheculed to receive if you stop earning a full-time wage. This calculation will help you as you plan ahead in order to generate adequate future income.

There are three forms to help you calculate your retirement income:

1. Social Security form

2. Company Retirement Benefits

3. Estimate of Retirement Income

III. Future Income upon Loss of Spouse

If you are married, estimate the impact on income of the loss of each spouse. This may be difficult emotionally to complete, but it is better to determine the financial facts now rather than later.

ESTIMATED BUDGET

GROSS INCOME PER MONTH _____

    Salary _____

    Interest _____

    Dividends _____

    Other (_____) _____

    Other (_____) _____

LESS:

1. **Tithe** _____

2. **Tax** (Est. - Incl. Fed., State, FICA) _____

NET SPENDABLE INCOME _____

3. **Housing** _____

    Mortgage (rent) _____

    Insurance _____

    Taxes _____

    Electricity _____

    Gas _____

    Water _____

    Sanitation _____

    Telephone _____

    Maintenance _____

    Other (_____) _____

    Other (_____) _____

4. **Food** _____

5. **Automobile(s)** _____

    Payments _____

    Gas and Oil _____

    Insurance _____

    License/Taxes _____

    Maint./Repair/Replace _____

6. **Insurance** _____

    Life _____

    Medical _____

    Other (_____) _____

7. **Debts** _____

    Credit Card _____

    Loans and Notes _____

    Other (_____) _____

    Other (_____) _____

8. **Enter./Recreation** _____

    Eating Out _____

    Baby Sitters _____

    Activities/Trips _____

    Vacation _____

    Other (_____) _____

    Other (_____) _____

9. **Clothing** _____

10. **Savings** _____

11. **Medical Expenses** _____

    Doctor _____

    Dentist _____

    Drugs _____

    Other (_____) _____

12. **Miscellaneous** _____

    Toiletry, cosmetics _____

    Beauty, barber _____

    Laundry, cleaning _____

    Allowances, lunches _____

    Subscriptions _____

    Gifts (incl. Christmas) _____

    Cash _____

    Cable/Internet _____

    Other (_____) _____

    Other (_____) _____

13. **Investments** _____

14. **School/Child Care** _____

    Tuition _____

    Materials _____

    Transportation _____

    Day Care _____

    Other (_____) _____

TOTAL EXPENSES _____

INCOME VERSUS EXPENSES

    Net Spendable Income _____

    Less Expenses _____

15. **Unallocated Surplus Income** [1] _____

[1] This category is used when surplus income is received. This would be kept in the checking account to be used within a few weeks; otherwise, it should be transferred to an allocated category.

SOCIAL SECURITY

Date_____

Social Security Number: _____

Location of Social Security Card: _____

Nearest Social Security Office:

Street Address: _____

City: _____ State: _____ Zip: _____

Telephone Number: _____

My (Our) Social Security Benefits Are as Follows: _____

_____

_____

_____

How to Determine Your Social Security Benefits

Facts about your Social Security benefits may be obtained by calling the Social Security Office toll-free (1-800-772-1213). If you are age 60 or older, you may obtain a benefits estimate by phone.

If you are under 60, you must request a form, which you will complete and mail back to the Social Security Office. Provide the Social Security Office your full name, your social security number and street address. Your earnings record will be sent along with other information about your possible benefits at various ages.

Telephone numbers and Social Security Regulations are subject to change. Please check your local telephone directory if the toll-free number noted above is not in service. Please note that you can now obtain this information on the Web at www.saa.gov.

How to File for Social Security Benefits upon Death of a Spouse

To receive Social Security benefits, go in person to the Social Security office as soon as possible after your spouse's death. A delay may void some of the benefits. When you go, take your spouse's Social Security card and death certificate. Also take your birth certificate, marriage certificate and birth certificates for each child.

COMPANY RETIREMENT BENEFITS

Date_____

Name of Company: _____

Address: _____

Telephone Number: _____

Department to Contact: _____

Name of Person to Contact: _____

Brief Description of Retirement Plan: _____

_____

_____

Monthly amount paid to beneficiary(s) at death, if any: _____

Lump sum amount paid to beneficiary(s) at death, if any: _____

Latest value of retirement plan: (date) _____ (amount) _____

Company booklet describing all benefits is located at: _____

_____

> *Please attach copy of the latest statement of Retirement Plan*

ESTIMATE OF RETIREMENT INCOME

Date_____

Source of Income	Amount of Monthly Income
Social Security	
Salary (Part-time/Full-time)	
Savings	
Investments	
Real Estate	
Business Income	
Veterans Benefits	
Company Retirement Benefits:	
Other:_____	
Other:_____	
Other:_____	

Total Monthly Income: →

FUTURE INCOME UPON LOSS OF A SPOUSE

Date_____

Following the loss of _____
the estimated monthly income for our family will be as follows:

Source of Income	Amount of Monthly Income
Survivor's Wage	
Social Security	
Savings and Investments	
Company Retirement Benefits	
Life Insurance Proceeds	
Earnings from Survivor's Employment	
Real Estate	
Other Income	
Total Income	
LESS: Monthly Spending	
SURPLUS OR DEFICIT	

---

*Consult your accountant or financial planner
to confirm the impact taxes will have on your income.*

FUTURE INCOME UPON LOSS OF A SPOUSE

Date_____

F ollowing the loss of _____
  the estimated monthly income for our family will be as follows:

Source of Income	Amount of Monthly Income
Survivor's Wage	
Social Security	
Savings and Investments	
Company Retirement Benefits	
Life Insurance Proceeds	
Earnings from Survivor's Employment	
Real Estate	
Other Income	
Total Income	
LESS: Monthly Spending	
SURPLUS OR DEFICIT	

Consult your accountant or financial planner
to confirm the impact taxes will have on your income.

ADVISORS / SAFE-DEPOSIT BOX / DEBT LIST / ACCOUNTS
Section Three

I. Advisors

Scripture encourages us to seek the counsel of wise, godly people. Proverbs 11:14 reads, *"Where there is no guidance, the people fall, but in abundance of counselors there is victory."*

In this section you will prepare a list of those who are your advisors. We have identified eight potential categories of counselors:

- Clergy
- Attorney
- Accountant
- Financial Advisor
- Insurance Agent
- Real Estate Advisor
- Banker
- Stock Broker

We have also provided a number of blank spaces for you to complete for those advisors who do not fit into these categories. There may be situations where you might use more than one person in a particular area. For example, you might have one accountant for your business and another for your personal tax preparation. You might need to identify business partners, investment clubs, affiliations, non-profit organizations or others with whom you have a significant relationship. Remember to complete this in pencil to be able to make changes easily. It is a good idea to attach the business card of each advisor.

II. Safe-Deposit Box

Now you will inventory your safe-deposit box, home safe, file cabinet and any other place you store important documents. This is a good time to "de-clutter" your storage area of items that no longer need to be in a secure place. Photocopy any documents that you want included in the Document Organizer you completed in Section Two.

There are three inventory forms in case you use more than one place for storage. Complete the inventory in pencil to allow for future changes.

III. Debt List

Many people don't know precisely what they owe. The Debt List will assist you in compiling your debts and the terms of each debt. The seven columns on the Debt List are as follows:

   1. Creditor — The one to whom the debt is owed.

   2. For what — Item purchased with the money borrowed.

   3. Monthly payment — The amount of the monthly payment. If payment is due more often than monthly, compute the total amount that is paid each month. For example, a $200 loan payment paid twice each month equals $400 per month. If payment is due less frequently than monthly, determine the average monthly cost. For example, a $600 payment paid twice a year would average $100 each month.

   4. Balance due — The amount of the outstanding debt.

   5. Scheduled pay-off date — The date by which the debt will be fully paid.

   6. Interest rate — The rate of interest charged for the debt.

   7. Payments past due — The number of payments, if any, past due on each debt.

After entering each debt, add and total the monthly payment and the balance due columns.

IV. Accounts

In addition to completing the Bank (or Security Company) and Credit Card Accounts forms, we also suggest that you place your credit cards on a copy machine and photocopy both sides of the cards. You might even consider copying everything you carry in your billfold and filing the copies in this section.

Be sure you record the emergency number to call and address to write if a credit card is lost or stolen.

Completing this section has encouraged some people to make positive changes. By canceling accounts and/or credit cards or consolidating two or more accounts into one, you may save bank charges, plus simplify your life. Changes in bank services may allow you to seek new kinds of accounts that will reduce bank charges or even pay you interest.

The last form in this section is a Computer Instruction form. This should be completed by those who have important financial data or personal information stored in computers.

A D V I S O R S

Date_____

Clergy:

Name: _____

Name of Church: _____

Street Address: _____

City, State, Zip: _____

Telephone Number: _____ FAX: _____

Attorney:

Name: _____

Name of Law Firm: _____

Street Address: _____

City, State, Zip: _____

Telephone Number: _____ FAX: _____

Accountant:

Name: _____

Name of Accounting Firm: _____

Street Address: _____

City, State, Zip: _____

Telephone Number: _____ FAX: _____

Financial Advisor:

Name: _____

Name of Company: _____

Street Address: _____

City, State, Zip: _____

Telephone Number: _____ FAX: _____

Insurance Agent:

Name: _____

Name of Agency: _____

Street Address: _____

City, State, Zip: _____

Telephone Number: _____ FAX: _____

Real Estate Advisor:

Name: _____

Name of Real Estate Company: _____

Street Address: _____

City, State, Zip: _____

Telephone Number: _____ FAX: _____

Banker:

Name: _____

Name of Bank: _____

Street Address: _____

City, State, Zip: _____

Telephone Number: _____ FAX: _____

Stock Broker:

Name: _____

Name of Brokerage Company: _____

Street Address: _____

City, State, Zip: _____

Telephone Number: _____ FAX: _____

Other _____:

Name: _____

Description of Relationship / Organization: _____

Street Address: _____

City, State, Zip: _____

Telephone Number: _____ FAX: _____

Other _____:

Name: _____

Description of Relationship / Organization: _____

Street Address: _____

City, State, Zip: _____

Telephone Number: _____ FAX: _____

Other _____:

Name: _____

Description of Relationship / Organization: _____

Street Address: _____

City, State, Zip: _____

Telephone Number: _____ FAX: _____

Other _____:

Name: _____

Description of Relationship / Organization: _____

Street Address: _____

City, State, Zip: _____

Telephone Number: _____ FAX: _____

SAFE-DEPOSIT BOX INVENTORY

Date_____

Location of Safe-Deposit Box or Other Secured Place: _____

Box Number: _____ Location of Keys: _____

Name of Financial Institution: _____

City, State, Zip: _____

Telephone Number: _____ FAX: _____

Those Authorized to Sign: _____

Inventory

Birth Certificates: _____

Marriage Certificates: _____

Social Security Cards: _____

Military Discharges: _____

Wills: _____

Trusts: _____

Deeds: _____

Mortgages: _____

Leases: _____

Business Agreements: _____

Investment Documents: _____

Automobile Titles: _____

Power of Attorney: _____

Insurance Policies: _____

Other: _____

_____

_____

_____

_____

_____

_____

SAFE-DEPOSIT BOX INVENTORY

Date_____

Location of Safe-Deposit Box or Other Secured Place: _____

Box Number: _____ Location of Keys: _____

Name of Financial Institution: _____

City, State, Zip: _____

Telephone Number: _____ FAX: _____

Those Authorized to Sign: _____

Inventory

Birth Certificates: _____

Marriage Certificates: _____

Social Security Cards: _____

Military Discharges: _____

Wills: _____

Trusts: _____

Deeds: _____

Mortgages: _____

Leases: _____

Business Agreements: _____

Investment Documents: _____

Automobile Titles: _____

Power of Attorney: _____

Insurance Policies: _____

Other: _____

_____

_____

_____

_____

_____

_____

HOME SAFE / FILE CABINET INVENTORY

Date_____

Location of Safe / File Cabinet: _____

Location of Keys or Combination: _____

Inventory

Birth Certificates: _____

Marriage Certificates: _____

Social Security Cards: _____

Military Discharges: _____

Wills: _____

Trusts: _____

Deeds: _____

Mortgages: _____

Leases: _____

Business Agreements: _____

Investment Documents: _____

Automobile Titles: _____

Power of Attorney: _____

Insurance Policies: _____

Other: _____

_____

_____

_____

_____

_____

_____

_____

_____

Creditor	Describe What Was Purchased	Monthly Payments	Balance Due	Scheduled Pay-Off Date	Interest Rate	Payments Past Due
Totals				/////		
Automobile Loans						
Total Automobile Loans				/////		
Home Mortgages						
Total Home Mortgages				/////		
Business Investments/Debt						
Total Business Investments				/////		

D E B T L I S T

Date: _____

BANK ACCOUNTS

Date_____

Account Name: _____

Account # _____ Name of Financial Institution: _____

Type of Account: Checking: ❏   Saving: ❏   Business: ❏   Interest Bearing: ❏

    Other (describe): _____   Joint Account: Yes ❏   No ❏

Those Authorized to Sign on Account:_____

Location of Checkbooks:_____

Account Name: _____

Account # _____ Name of Financial Institution: _____

Type of Account: Checking: ❏   Saving: ❏   Business: ❏   Interest Bearing: ❏

    Other (describe): _____   Joint Account: Yes ❏   No ❏

Those Authorized to Sign on Account:_____

Location of Checkbooks:_____

Account Name: _____

Account # _____ Name of Financial Institution: _____

Type of Account: Checking: ❏   Saving: ❏   Business: ❏   Interest Bearing: ❏

    Other (describe): _____   Joint Account: Yes ❏   No ❏

Those Authorized to Sign on Account:_____

Location of Checkbooks:_____

Account Name: _____

Account # _____ Name of Financial Institution: _____

Type of Account: Checking: ❏   Saving: ❏   Business: ❏   Interest Bearing: ❏

    Other (describe): _____   Joint Account: Yes ❏   No ❏

Those Authorized to Sign on Account:_____

Location of Checkbooks:_____

CREDIT CARDS

Card Issued By: _____ #: _____

Those Authorized to Sign on Card: _____

Location of Card(s): _____

If Lost/Stolen, Call: _____ Write: _____

Card Issued By: _____ #: _____

Those Authorized to Sign on Card: _____

Location of Card(s): _____

If Lost/Stolen, Call: _____ Write: _____

Card Issued By: _____ #: _____

Those Authorized to Sign on Card: _____

Location of Card(s): _____

If Lost/Stolen, Call: _____ Write: _____

Card Issued By: _____ #: _____

Those Authorized to Sign on Card: _____

Location of Card(s): _____

If Lost/Stolen, Call: _____ Write: _____

Card Issued By: _____ #: _____

Those Authorized to Sign on Card: _____

Location of Card(s): _____

If Lost/Stolen, Call: _____ Write: _____

Card Issued By: _____ #: _____

Those Authorized to Sign on Card: _____

Location of Card(s): _____

If Lost/Stolen, Call: _____ Write: _____

COMPUTER INSTRUCTIONS

Date_____

Location of Computers: _____

_____

Name of Programs Containing Important Information

Name of Program Files Containing Information

_____   _____

_____   _____

_____   _____

_____   _____

_____   _____

_____   _____

_____   _____

_____   _____

_____   _____

Person(s) familiar with our computer and programs who can retrieve what is needed:

Name: _____

Company Name: _____

Address: _____

Telephone Number: _____

Name: _____

Company Name: _____

Address: _____

Telephone Number: _____

T he asset inventory is one of the most important sections and for many people it requires the most time to complete.

Attach copies of the monthly account statements provided by the financial institutions or brokerage companies that are custodians of your savings and investments. At the top of each statement identify the person to contact, their phone number and address.

In addition to the assets identified on these statements, you may have other assets. Complete the appropriate forms. If possible, attach a photocopy of the document or title for each asset (stock certificates, real estate deeds, car titles, etc.).

Complete the following forms:

1. **Automobiles and Other Vehicles**

2. **Valuable Personal Property**

Those who have valuable property, such as coins, stamps, musical instruments, camera equipment and computers, may choose to document these items in detail on this form.

Every time you purchase furniture, appliances or other expensive personal property, file the bill of sale in case you ever need to substantiate the value of an item. To inventory the rest of your personal property, we suggest you go through your home room-by-room and list each item. Place this list in this section of the notebook.

One of the easiest and most effective ways to inventory your personal and household possessions is to videotape them. Describe the articles, including the information about purchase dates and costs if known. Date the tape. Because this video tape documents your possessions in case of fire, theft or other possible loss, we suggest that you make two tapes and store one of them in a safe-deposit box or other secure location away from your home .

3. **Stocks which you hold (not held by a custodian)**

4. **Bonds which you hold (not held by a custodian)**

5. **Other securities / Mutual funds**

6. **Other investments**

7. **Receivables**

8. **Real estate**

If you need additional forms, please photocopy as many as necessary.

Description of Vehicle: _____

Registered Owner(s): _____

Owner's Address: _____

Make of Vehicle: _____ Body Type: _____ Lic.No./State: _____

Identification #: _____ Title: _____

First Lien Holder: _____

Second Lien Holder: _____

Description of Vehicle: _____

Registered Owner(s): _____

Owner's Address: _____

Make of Vehicle: _____ Body Type: _____ Lic.No./State: _____

Identification #: _____ Title: _____

First Lien Holder: _____

Second Lien Holder: _____

Description of Vehicle: _____

Registered Owner(s): _____

Owner's Address: _____

Make of Vehicle: _____ Body Type: _____ Lic.No./State: _____

Identification #: _____ Title: _____

First Lien Holder: _____

Second Lien Holder: _____

Place a copy of each vehicle's title and registration form in this workbook.

Date_____

Description of Vehicle: _____

Registered Owner(s): _____

Owner's Address: _____

Make of Vehicle: _____ Body Type: _____ Lic.No./State: _____

Identification #: _____ Title: _____

First Lien Holder: _____

Second Lien Holder: _____

Description of Vehicle: _____

Registered Owner(s): _____

Owner's Address: _____

Make of Vehicle: _____ Body Type: _____ Lic.No./State: _____

Identification #: _____ Title: _____

First Lien Holder: _____

Second Lien Holder: _____

Description of Vehicle: _____

Registered Owner(s): _____

Owner's Address: _____

Make of Vehicle: _____ Body Type: _____ Lic.No./State: _____

Identification #: _____ Title: _____

First Lien Holder: _____

Second Lien Holder: _____

Place a copy of each vehicle's title and registration form in this workbook.

VALUABLE PERSONAL PROPERTY

Date_____

The following are the descriptions and estimated values of some of our most valuable property:

Description of Property:_____

Estimated Value: _____ Date of Value: _____ Appraised: Yes ❑   No ❑

Description of Property:_____

Estimated Value: _____ Date of Value: _____ Appraised: Yes ❑   No ❑

Description of Property:_____

Estimated Value: _____ Date of Value: _____ Appraised: Yes ❑   No ❑

Description of Property:_____

 Estimated Value: _____ Date of Value: _____ Appraised: Yes ❑   No ❑

Description of Property:_____

Estimated Value: _____ Date of Value: _____ Appraised: Yes ❑   No ❑

Description of Property:_____

Estimated Value: _____ Date of Value: _____ Appraised: Yes ❑   No ❑

Description of Property:_____

Estimated Value: _____ Date of Value: _____ Appraised: Yes ❑   No ❑

Description of Property:_____

Estimated Value: _____ Date of Value: _____ Appraised: Yes ❑   No ❑

Description of Property:_____

Estimated Value: _____ Date of Value: _____ Appraised: Yes ❑   No ❑

> *Please ask your insurance agent to determine if these items are properly covered in your household or other insurance policies and if the coverages reflect current values. Attach photocopies of any appraisals.*

STOCKS WHICH YOU HOLD

Date_____

Description of Stock: _____
Number of Shares: _____ Dividend Information: _____
Date Acquired: _____ Purchase Price: _____
Where Held: _____ Other Information: _____

Description of Stock: _____
Number of Shares: _____ Dividend Information: _____
Date Acquired: _____ Purchase Price: _____
Where Held: _____ Other Information: _____

Description of Stock: _____
Number of Shares: _____ Dividend Information: _____
Date Acquired: _____ Purchase Price: _____
Where Held: _____ Other Information: _____

Description of Stock: _____
Number of Shares: _____ Dividend Information: _____
Date Acquired: _____ Purchase Price: _____
Where Held: _____ Other Information: _____

Description of Stock: _____
Number of Shares: _____ Dividend Information: _____
Date Acquired: _____ Purchase Price: _____
Where Held: _____ Other Information: _____

Description of Stock: _____
Number of Shares: _____ Dividend Information: _____
Date Acquired: _____ Purchase Price: _____
Where Held: _____ Other Information: _____

Description of Stock: _____
Number of Shares: _____ Dividend Information: _____
Date Acquired: _____ Purchase Price: _____
Where Held: _____ Other Information: _____

BONDS WHICH YOU HOLD

Date_____

Description of Bond: _____

Face Amount: _____ Yield: _____ Maturity Date: _____

Date Acquired: _____ Purchase Price: _____

Where Held: _____ Other Information: _____

Description of Bond: _____

Face Amount: _____ Yield: _____ Maturity Date: _____

Other Information: _____

Date Acquired: _____ Purchase Price: _____

Where Held: _____ Other Information: _____

Description of Bond: _____

Face Amount: _____ Yield: _____ Maturity Date: _____

Other Information: _____

Date Acquired: _____ Purchase Price: _____

Where Held: _____ Other Information: _____

Description of Bond: _____

Face Amount: _____ Yield: _____ Maturity Date: _____

Other Information: _____

Date Acquired: _____ Purchase Price: _____

Where Held: _____ Other Information: _____

Description of Bond: _____

Face Amount: _____ Yield: _____ Maturity Date: _____

Other Information: _____

Date Acquired: _____ Purchase Price: _____

Where Held: _____ Other Information: _____

Description of Bond: _____

Face Amount: _____ Yield: _____ Maturity Date: _____

Other Information: _____

Date Acquired: _____ Purchase Price: _____

Where Held: _____ Other Information: _____

OTHER SECURITIES / MUTUAL FUNDS

Date_____

Name and Description: _____

_____

Person to Contact (if applicable): _____ Telephone #: _____

Address: _____

Date Acquired: _____ Purchase Price: _____

Where Held: _____ Other Information: _____

Name and Description: _____

_____

Person to Contact (if applicable): _____ Telephone #: _____

Address: _____

Date Acquired: _____ Purchase Price: _____

Where Held: _____ Other Information: _____

Name and Description: _____

_____

Person to Contact (if applicable): _____ Telephone #: _____

Address: _____

Date Acquired: _____ Purchase Price: _____

Where Held: _____ Other Information: _____

Name and Description: _____

_____

Person to Contact (if applicable): _____ Telephone #: _____

Address: _____

Date Acquired: _____ Purchase Price: _____

Where Held: _____ Other Information: _____

Name and Description: _____

_____

Person to Contact (if applicable): _____ Telephone #: _____

Address: _____

Date Acquired: _____ Purchase Price: _____

Where Held: _____ Other Information: _____

OTHER INVESTMENTS

Date_____

Name and Description of Investment: _____

_____

Person to Contact (if applicable): _____ Telephone #: _____

Address: _____

Date Acquired: _____ Purchase Price: _____

Name and Description of Investment: _____

_____

Person to Contact (if applicable): _____ Telephone #: _____

Address: _____

Date Acquired: _____ Purchase Price: _____

Name and Description of Investment: _____

_____

Person to Contact (if applicable): _____ Telephone #: _____

Address: _____

Date Acquired: _____ Purchase Price: _____

Name and Description of Investment: _____

_____

Person to Contact (if applicable): _____ Telephone #: _____

Address: _____

Date Acquired: _____ Purchase Price: _____

Name and Description of Investment: _____

_____

Person to Contact (if applicable): _____ Telephone #: _____

Address: _____

Date Acquired: _____ Purchase Price: _____

Name and Description of Investment: _____

_____

Person to Contact (if applicable): _____ Telephone #: _____

Address: _____

Date Acquired: _____ Purchase Price: _____

Date_____

Debtor's Name: _____ Telephone: _____

Address: _____

Loan Amount: _____ Terms of Payment: _____

_____

Location of Agreement: _____

Additional Terms or Information: _____

_____

Debtor's Name: _____ Telephone: _____

Address: _____

Loan Amount: _____ Terms of Payment: _____

_____

Location of Agreement: _____

Additional Terms or Information: _____

_____

Debtor's Name: _____ Telephone: _____

Address: _____

Loan Amount: _____ Terms of Payment: _____

_____

Location of Agreement: _____

Additional Terms or Information: _____

_____

Debtor's Name: _____ Telephone: _____

Address: _____

Loan Amount: _____ Terms of Payment: _____

_____

Location of Agreement: _____

Additional Terms or Information: _____

_____

R E A L   E S T A T E

Description: _____

Location of Property: _____

Deed in Name(s) of: _____

Purchase Price: _____ Purchase Date: _____

Location of Deed: _____

Assessed Value: (Land) _____ (Building) _____ (Total) _____

Other Taxes/Assessments Due: (Amount) _____ (Date Payable) _____

Mortgage Holder: _____

Mortgage Satisfaction (if fully paid) is Located: _____

Lease/Rental Agreement (if rental property) is Located: _____

Terms of Lease/Rental Agreement: _____

_____

Description: _____

Location of Property: _____

Deed in Name(s) of: _____

Purchase Price: _____ Purchase Date: _____

Location of Deed: _____

Assessed Value: (Land) _____ (Building) _____ (Total) _____

Other Taxes/Assessments Due: (Amount) _____ (Date Payable) _____

Mortgage Holder: _____

Mortgage Satisfaction (if fully paid) is Located: _____

Lease/Rental Agreement (if rental property) is Located: _____

Terms of Lease/Rental Agreement: _____

_____

R E A L   E S T A T E

Date_____

Description: _____

Location of Property: _____

Deed in Name(s) of: _____

Purchase Price: _____ Purchase Date: _____

Location of Deed: _____

Assessed Value: (Land) _____ (Building) _____ (Total) _____

Other Taxes/Assessments Due: (Amount) _____ (Date Payable) _____

Mortgage Holder: _____

Mortgage Satisfaction (if fully paid) is Located: _____

Lease/Rental Agreement (if rental property) is Located: _____

Terms of Lease/Rental Agreement: _____

_____

Description: _____

Location of Property: _____

Deed in Name(s) of: _____

Purchase Price: _____ Purchase Date: _____

Location of Deed: _____

Assessed Value: (Land) _____ (Building) _____ (Total) _____

Other Taxes/Assessments Due: (Amount) _____ (Date Payable) _____

Mortgage Holder: _____

Mortgage Satisfaction (if fully paid) is Located: _____

Lease/Rental Agreement (if rental property) is Located: _____

Terms of Lease/Rental Agreement: _____

_____

I N S U R A N C E
Section Five

I n this section you will organize your insurance. The area of insurance can be confusing. Consequently, most people do not know all they should about their insurance, and rarely is it properly organized.

One reason this area can be confusing is because there are so many different types of insurance. The following is a partial list of various types of insurance:

- Life
- Health
- Disability
- Automobile
- Homeowner's

- Dental
- Liability Umbrella
- Tenant
- Household Possessions
- Jewelry

First, gather all your insurance policies together. Check carefully to be certain the coverage, the beneficiaries and the values of all policies are accurate and current. *We recommend a review of policies with a trusted advisor and your insurance agent to confirm that you have the best insurance products for your needs and budget.*

Complete the Insurance Inventory.

Then, photocopy the title pages of all policies and file them in the Document Organizer or in this notebook. This way you will always have ready access to the important information in each policy. We suggest that you store the originals in your safe-deposit box or in another secure location.

If you are covered by some type of insurance where you work, complete the Work Related Insurance form.

INSURANCE INVENTORY

Date_____

LIFE INSURANCE

Insurance Company: _____ Person Insured: _____

Insurance Agent: _____ Telephone Number: _____

Address: _____

Beneficiary: _____ Policy Number: _____

Premium Due Date: _____ Premium Payment: _____

Value: _____ Face Amount: _____ Cash Value: _____

LIFE INSURANCE

Insurance Company: _____ Person Insured: _____

Insurance Agent: _____ Telephone Number: _____

Address: _____

Beneficiary: _____ Policy Number: _____

Premium Due Date: _____ Premium Payment: _____

Value: _____ Face Amount: _____ Cash Value: _____

LIFE INSURANCE

Insurance Company: _____ Person Insured: _____

Insurance Agent: _____ Telephone Number: _____

Address: _____

Beneficiary: _____ Policy Number: _____

Premium Due Date: _____ Premium Payment: _____

Value: _____ Face Amount: _____ Cash Value: _____

HOMEOWNER'S (TENANT'S) INSURANCE

Insurance Company: _____

Insurance Agent: _____ Telephone Number: _____

Address: _____

Property Covered: _____ Policy Number: _____

Coverage: _____

Premium Due Date: _____ Premium Payment: _____

AUTOMOBILE INSURANCE

Insurance Company: _____

Insurance Agent: _____ Telephone Number: _____

Address: _____

Vehicle Covered: _____ Policy Number: _____

Coverage: _____

Premium Due Date: _____ Premium Payment: _____

Insurance Company: _____

Insurance Agent: _____ Telephone Number: _____

Address: _____

Vehicle Covered: _____ Policy Number: _____

Coverage: _____

Premium Due Date: _____ Premium Payment: _____

LIABILITY INSURANCE

Insurance Company: _____

Insurance Agent: _____

Address: _____

Telephone Number: _____

Person(s) Covered: _____

Policy Number: _____

Coverage: _____

Premium Due Date: _____ Premium Payment: _____

HEALTH INSURANCE

Insurance Company: _____ Person Insured: _____

Insurance Agent: _____ Telephone Number: _____

Address: _____

Person(s) Covered: _____ Policy Number: _____

Coverage: _____

Premium Due Date: _____ Premium Payment: _____

DISABILITY INSURANCE

Insurance Company: _____ Person Insured: _____

Insurance Agent: _____ Telephone Number: _____

Address: _____

Person(s) Covered: _____ Policy Number: _____

Coverage: _____

Premium Due Date: _____ Premium Payment: _____

OTHER INSURANCE

Insurance Company: _____ Person Insured: _____

Insurance Agent: _____ Telephone Number: _____

Address: _____

Person(s) Covered: _____ Policy Number: _____

Coverage: _____

Premium Due Date: _____ Premium Payment: _____

Insurance Company: _____ Person Insured: _____

Insurance Agent: _____ Telephone Number: _____

Address: _____

Person(s) Covered: _____ Policy Number: _____

Coverage: _____

Premium Due Date: _____ Premium Payment: _____

WORK RELATED INSURANCE

Date_____

Name of Company Where I Work: _____

Address: _____

Telephone Number: _____

Name of Person or Department to Contact: _____

Life Insurance Company: _____

Insurance Company Address: _____

Dollar Amount: _____ Accidental Death Amount: _____

Method of Payment: _____

Name of Person to Contact: _____

Policy Number: _____

Health Insurance Company : _____

Insurance Company Address: _____

Telephone Number: _____

Policy Number: _____

Name of Person to Contact: _____

Summary of Policy: _____

Disability Insurance Company: _____

Insurance Company Address: _____

Telephone Number: _____

Policy Number: _____

Name of Person to Contact: _____

Summary of Policy: _____

> *Attach copy of Summary of Benefits from Policy or Employee Handbook*

Dental Insurance Company: _____

    Insurance Company Address: _____

    Dollar Amount: _____ Accidental Death Amount: _____

    Method of Payment: _____

    Name of Person to Contact: _____

    Policy Number: _____

Cancer Insurance Company : _____

    Insurance Company Address: _____

    Telephone Number: _____

    Policy Number: _____

    Name of Person to Contact: _____

    Summary of Policy: _____

_____ Company: _____

    Insurance Company Address: _____

    Telephone Number: _____

    Policy Number: _____

    Name of Person to Contact: _____

    Summary of Policy: _____

> *Attach copy of Summary of Benefits from Policy or Employee Handbook*

ESTATE DOCUMENTS
Section Six

I n this section you will organize your Estate Documents and complete your Funeral Instructions.

I.   Estate Documents

A tremendous gift to your loved ones is a thoughtfully prepared will. Your attorney and accountant may advise you to execute other necessary estate documents such as trusts or a power-of-attorney.

If you have a will, trust, power-of-attorney, or other estate documents, use a copy machine with reduction capabilities to reduce the documents to a letter size, 8-1/2 x 11 inches. Insert them in this section of the notebook. The originals should be stored in a secure place.

If you do not yet have any of these documents, please read this carefully:

Why should you have a will? A will is necessary to enable you to distribute your property according to your wishes after your death. Without a will or proper estate documents, the laws of your state will determine the distribution.

It is hard to believe that three out of four people die without a will! Many who have a will admit it needs to be updated because of changing circumstances. You need to consider revising your estate documents when:

- Additional children have been born or adopted.

- You have moved to a different state

- Your financial affairs have changed.

- Your marital status has changed.

- A beneficiary has died.

- Tax laws have changed.

- Your attorney or accountant suggests doing so.

Preparing estate documents takes time. We strongly recommend that you seek the counsel of a competent attorney and accountant who are experienced in the preparation of estate documents. On page 67 is a checklist of potential estate documents you may want or need.

II.   Distribution of Household Possessions

The distribution of most major assets should be accomplished by an estate document, such as a will or a trust. Most people, however, do not contemplate how they should distribute the remaining personal property such as household goods, automobiles, clothes, books, pictures, family slides, tools and china. This may be done in one of these ways:

1. **You designate every item.**

In a will, trust or other estate document you would designate the personal property each beneficiary would receive.

2. **You designate some items and establish "ground rules" for the remaining items.**

Designate a portion of the personal property in the estate document. The remainder would be distributed to your heirs based on a system you choose. An example would be: "The remaining properties will be divided among the heirs in equal portions. Start with the oldest child and have each heir alternately choose the article they would like to have among the items that remain until everything has been distributed.

3. **You designate no items, but you establish the "ground rules."**

III. Funeral Instructions

Next, draft Funeral and Burial Instructions. Remember, this will be an emotional time for your loved ones, and these instructions will help them make good decisions. There are two copies of the instructions — one for you and one for your spouse if you are married. If other family members also want to complete their funeral and burial instructions, they may photocopy the form for their use.

IMPORTANT NOTICE!

This workbook is intended to serve as an aid in assembling your financial data. No decisions made concerning insurance, investments, ownership of assets, estate planning and any legal documents should be made without the advice and assistance of competent legal, tax and estate professionals.

ESTATE DOCUMENTS CHECKLIST

Date_____

Name of Document	Person(s) Covered By Document	Document Is Current	Needs Revision	Need, But Do Not Have
Will				
Will				
Trust				
Trust				
Power-of-Attorney				
Power-of-Attorney				
Living Will				
Other Documents:				

FUNERAL INSTRUCTIONS

Date_____

These Are the Wishes of: (Name) _____

Funeral Home Preference:

Name: _____

Address: _____

Telephone Number: _____

Person to Contact at Funeral Home: _____

Description of any arrangements you have made with the funeral home: _____

_____

_____

_____

_____

_____

Viewing Wishes:

Open Casket: ❑   Closed Casket: ❑

Location of Service:

Name of Church or Funeral Home: _____

Address: _____

Requests for Funeral Service:

Name of Minister:_____

Description of Service: _____

_____

_____

_____

_____

Musical Selections: _____

Organist: Yes ❑ No ❑   Pianist: Yes ❑ No ❑   Vocalist: Yes ❑ No ❑

Special Requests: (biblical passages, clothing, etc.): _____

_____

_____

_____

_____

_____

Interment:

Name of Cemetery: _____

Address: _____

Location of Cemetery Lot(s):

Legal Description: Lot # [＿＿＿]   Block # [＿＿＿]   Section # [＿＿＿]

Casket:

I would like the following type of casket: _____

_____

_____

_____

Pall Bearers:

I would like the following pall bearers: _____

_____

_____

Cremation: ❏   Yes   ❏   No

If you choose to be cremated, describe what you would like done with your ashes.

_____

_____

_____

_____

Memorial:

I would like flowers: Yes ❏ No ❏ If no, in lieu of flowers please make contributions to the following organizations:

1. _____

2. _____

3. _____

4. _____

Donor's Information: I wish ❏ do not wish ❏ to make an anatomical gift, to take effect upon my death. If you do wish to make such a gift, we recommend you make a copy of the document and include it in this section. Keep the original in a secure place.

Signed: _____   **Dated:** _____

FUNERAL INSTRUCTIONS

Date_____

These Are the Wishes of: (Name) _____

Funeral Home Preference:

Name: _____

Address: _____

Telephone Number: _____

Person to Contact at Funeral Home: _____

Description of any arrangements you have made with the funeral home: _____

_____

_____

_____

_____

_____

Viewing Wishes:

Open Casket: ❑   Closed Casket: ❑

Location of Service:

Name of Church or Funeral Home: _____

Address: _____

Requests for Funeral Service:

Name of Minister: _____

Description of Service: _____

_____

_____

_____

_____

Musical Selections: _____

Organist: Yes ❑ No ❑   Pianist: Yes ❑ No ❑   Vocalist: Yes ❑ No ❑

Special Requests: (biblical passages, clothing, etc.): _____

_____

_____

_____

_____

_____

Interment:

Name of Cemetery: _____

Address: _____

Location of Cemetery Lot(s):

Legal Description: Lot # [   ]   Block # [   ]   Section # [   ]

Casket:

I would like the following type of casket: _____

_____

_____

_____

Pall Bearers:

I would like the following pall bearers: _____

_____

_____

Cremation: ❑ Yes   ❑ No

If you choose to be cremated, describe what you would like done with your ashes.

_____

_____

_____

_____

Memorial:

I would like flowers: Yes ❑ No ❑ If no, in lieu of flowers please make contributions to the following organizations:

1. _____

2. _____

3. _____

4. _____

Donor's Information: I wish ❑ do not wish ❑ to make an anatomical gift, to take effect upon my death. If you do wish to make such a gift, we recommend you make a copy of the document and include it in this section. Keep the original in a secure place.

Signed: _____   **Dated:** _____

FAMILY / OPTIONAL IDEAS
Section Seven

I n this section you and your family members, if any, will complete your Personal History. The purpose of this exercise is to gather in one place information you will need to know about those in your family.

I. Family

There are four blank Personal History forms. One for you, one for your spouse, if you are married, and two for other family members. If you need additional forms, please photocopy as many as you need. We suggest that you and your spouse complete your forms in detail. Then complete the Personal History forms for the other members of your family only in the detail that you need.

Leaving a Family History

Throughout Scripture there are examples of godly people leaving their descendants a history of their families. For instance, the genealogy of Jesus Christ is recounted in Matthew 1:1-17.

We encourage you to leave your family this legacy. There are a number of alternatives from which you may choose. You may decide to leave your family history in writing or on an audio or video tape.

This is a wonderful opportunity to communicate to future generations your life story — including a description of how you were introduced to Jesus Christ and a chronicle of your life's journey with Him.

II. Optional Ideas

The following ideas can be very helpful. You are **not required** to complete this section.

1. Helpful Household Answers. If this information is readily accessible, it can be important in case of an emergency. It also is very helpful for baby-sitters, older teens and house guests. We suggest that you place a photocopy of this form in a clear plastic holder and post it near your telephone.

2. Major Home Improvements. Major home improvements add value to your home and, if you keep an accurate record of them, may save taxes when you sell your home. Examples of these home improvements are: adding landscaping, a sprinkler system or building a pool. File the paid invoices and checks for these improvements in your Document Organizer.

3. Items Loaned to Others. How many times have you loaned something to a friend and then forgotten who was the borrower? This form is designed to help you keep track of items you loan.

4. When Your Marital Status Changes. A helpful checklist of changes that need to be made in the event of marriage, divorce or death of a spouse.

5. Incompetence, Disability or Remarriage. These issues can be highly emotional and difficult to discuss. We have included them only to stimulate your thinking.

6. Memo to Loved Ones. We recommend that you write a memo or letter to your loved ones telling them why you provided this workbook. A sample memo is enclosed for your review.

CONCLUSION

By completing this notebook, you have loved your family in a tangible way. Review the notebook with your loved ones. **Show them where you keep it.**

Every time something happens which changes any of this information, turn to the proper page and make a revision. Make a note on your calendar to review the entire notebook every six months. Usually you'll be surprised at how many things have changed.

PERSONAL HISTORY

Date_____

Name: _____

Marital Status: Married ❑ Single ❑ Widowed ❑ Divorced ❑

Street Address: _____

City: _____ State: _____ Zip: _____

Date of Birth: _____ Birthplace: _____

Birth Certificate Location: _____

Citizenship: USA Yes ❑ No ❑ If no, describe: _____

Social Security Number: _____ Phone Number: _____

Spouse's Name: _____

Date of Birth:_____Birthplace:_____Social Security #: _____

Citizenship: USA Yes ❑ No ❑ If no, describe: _____

Spouse's Social Security Number: _____

Father's Name: _____

Date of Birth:_____Birthplace:_____Social Security #: _____

Mother's Name: _____

Date of Birth:_____Birthplace:_____Social Security #: _____

Education: Name of School: _____

Address: _____

Degree: _____

Date: _____

Military Service: Branch of Service: _____

Serial Number: _____

Enlistment Date: _____ Discharge Date: _____ Rank: _____

Military Honors: _____

Fraternal, Service and Social Memberships: _____

_____

_____

Special Recognitions: _____

_____

Church: Name _____

Address: _____

Employment: Job Title and Description _____ _____

Company Name: _____

Address: _____

First Child's Name: _____

Date of Birth: _____ Birthplace: _____

Birth Certificate Location: _____ Social Security #: _____

Address: _____

Second Child's Name: _____

Date of Birth: _____ Birthplace: _____

Birth Certificate Location: _____ Social Security #: _____

Address: _____

Third Child's Name: _____

Date of Birth: _____ Birthplace: _____

Birth Certificate Location: _____ Social Security #: _____

Address: _____

Fourth Child's Name: _____

Date of Birth: _____ Birthplace: _____

Birth Certificate Location: _____ Social Security #: _____

Address: _____

PERSONAL HISTORY

Date_____

Name: _____

Marital Status: Married ☐ Single ☐ Widowed ☐ Divorced ☐

Street Address: _____

City: _____ State: _____ Zip: _____

Date of Birth: _____ Birthplace: _____

Birth Certificate Location: _____

Citizenship: USA Yes ☐ No ☐ If no, describe: _____

Social Security Number: _____ Phone Number: _____

Spouse's Name: _____

Date of Birth:_____Birthplace:_____Social Security #: _____

Citizenship: USA Yes ☐ No ☐ If no, describe: _____

Spouse's Social Security Number: _____

Father's Name: _____

Date of Birth:_____Birthplace:_____Social Security #: _____

Mother's Name: _____

Date of Birth:_____Birthplace:_____Social Security #: _____

Education: Name of School: _____

Address: _____

Degree: _____

Date: _____

Military Service: Branch of Service: _____

Serial Number: _____

Enlistment Date: _____ Discharge Date: _____ Rank: _____

Military Honors: _____

Fraternal, Service and Social Memberships: _____

_____

_____

Special Recognitions: _____

_____

Church: Name _____

Address: _____

Employment: Job Title and Description _____

Company Name: _____

Address: _____

First Child's Name: _____

Date of Birth: _____ Birthplace: _____

Birth Certificate Location: _____ Social Security #: _____

Address: _____

Second Child's Name: _____

Date of Birth: _____ Birthplace: _____

Birth Certificate Location: _____ Social Security #: _____

Address: _____

Third Child's Name: _____

Date of Birth: _____ Birthplace: _____

Birth Certificate Location: _____ Social Security #: _____

Address: _____

Fourth Child's Name: _____

Date of Birth: _____ Birthplace: _____

Birth Certificate Location: _____ Social Security #: _____

Address: _____

PERSONAL HISTORY

Date_____

Name: _____

Marital Status: Married ❑   Single ❑   Widowed ❑   Divorced ❑

Street Address: _____

City: _____   State: _____   Zip: _____

Date of Birth: _____   Birthplace: _____

Birth Certificate Location: _____

Citizenship: USA Yes ❑   No ❑   If no, describe: _____

Social Security Number: _____   Phone Number: _____

Spouse's Name: _____

Date of Birth:_____Birthplace:_____Social Security #: _____

Citizenship: USA Yes ❑   No ❑   If no, describe: _____

Spouse's Social Security Number: _____

Father's Name: _____

Date of Birth:_____Birthplace:_____Social Security #: _____

Mother's Name: _____

Date of Birth:_____Birthplace:_____Social Security #: _____

Education: Name of School: _____

Address: _____

Degree: _____

Date: _____

Military Service: Branch of Service: _____

Serial Number: _____

Enlistment Date: _____   Discharge Date: _____   Rank: _____

Military Honors: _____

Fraternal, Service and Social Memberships: _____
_____
_____

Special Recognitions: _____
_____

Church: Name _____

Address: _____

Employment: Job Title and Description _____

Company Name: _____

Address: _____

First Child's Name: _____

Date of Birth: _____ Birthplace: _____

Birth Certificate Location: _____ Social Security #: _____

Address: _____

Second Child's Name: _____

Date of Birth: _____ Birthplace: _____

Birth Certificate Location: _____ Social Security #: _____

Address: _____

Third Child's Name: _____

Date of Birth: _____ Birthplace: _____

Birth Certificate Location: _____ Social Security #: _____

Address: _____

Fourth Child's Name: _____

Date of Birth: _____ Birthplace: _____

Birth Certificate Location: _____ Social Security #: _____

Address: _____

PERSONAL HISTORY

Date_____

Name: _____

Marital Status: Married ☐ Single ☐ Widowed ☐ Divorced ☐

Street Address: _____

City: _____ State: _____ Zip: _____

Date of Birth: _____ Birthplace: _____

Birth Certificate Location: _____

Citizenship: USA Yes ☐ No ☐ If no, describe: _____

Social Security Number: _____ Phone Number: _____

Spouse's Name: _____

Date of Birth:_____Birthplace:_____Social Security #: _____

Citizenship: USA Yes ☐ No ☐ If no, describe: _____

Spouse's Social Security Number: _____

Father's Name: _____

Date of Birth:_____Birthplace:_____Social Security #: _____

Mother's Name: _____

Date of Birth:_____Birthplace:_____Social Security #: _____

Education: Name of School: _____

Address: _____

Degree: _____

Date: _____

Military Service: Branch of Service: _____

Serial Number: _____

Enlistment Date: _____ Discharge Date: _____ Rank: _____

Military Honors: _____

Fraternal, Service and Social Memberships: _____
_____
_____

Special Recognitions: _____
_____

Church: Name _____

Address: _____

Employment: Job Title and Description _____

Company Name: _____

Address: _____

First Child's Name: _____

Date of Birth: _____ Birthplace: _____

Birth Certificate Location: _____ Social Security #: _____

Address: _____

Second Child's Name: _____

Date of Birth: _____ Birthplace: _____

Birth Certificate Location: _____ Social Security #: _____

Address: _____

Third Child's Name: _____

Date of Birth: _____ Birthplace: _____

Birth Certificate Location: _____ Social Security #: _____

Address: _____

Fourth Child's Name: _____

Date of Birth: _____ Birthplace: _____

Birth Certificate Location: _____ Social Security #: _____

Address: _____

HELPFUL HOUSEHOLD ANSWERS

Date_____

Home Address: _____ Phone: _____

Vehicles:

Vehicle Make:_____ Model: _____ Color: _____ License #: _____

Vehicle Make:_____ Model: _____ Color: _____ License #: _____

Vehicle Make:_____ Model: _____ Color: _____ License #: _____

Neighbor: Name _____ Home Phone: _____

Work Phone: _____Address: _____

Relative: Name: _____ Home Phone: _____

Work Phone: _____Address: _____

Location of: Extra House Key: _____

                 Electrical Breaker: _____

                 Water Cut-off: _____

                 Thermostat: _____

                 Alarm System Box: _____

                 Fire Extinguisher: _____

                 Other: _____

Helpful Names and Numbers:

Alarm Company: _____ Phone: _____

Doctor: _____ Phone: _____

Hospital: _____ Phone: _____

Dentist: _____ Phone: _____

Drug Store: _____ Phone: _____

Veterinarian: _____ Phone: _____

Electrician: _____ Phone: _____

Plumber: _____ Phone: _____

Air/Heating: _____ Phone: _____

Appliance Repair: _____ Phone: _____

Clergy: _____ Phone: _____

Fire Department: _____ Phone: _____

Police Department: _____ Phone: _____

MAJOR HOME IMPROVEMENTS
(Since Purchase of Home)

Date	Description	Cost	Total-to-Date

ITEMS LOANED TO OTHERS

We have loaned the following items to others:

Item: _____   Loaned To: _____

Borrower's Phone #: _____   Date Item Is To Be Returned: _____

Item: _____   Loaned To: _____

Borrower's Phone #: _____   Date Item Is To Be Returned: _____

Item: _____   Loaned To: _____

Borrower's Phone #: _____   Date Item Is To Be Returned: _____

Item: _____   Loaned To: _____

Borrower's Phone #: _____   Date Item Is To Be Returned: _____

Item: _____   Loaned To: _____

Borrower's Phone #: _____   Date Item Is To Be Returned: _____

Item: _____   Loaned To: _____

Borrower's Phone #: _____   Date Item Is To Be Returned: _____

Item: _____   Loaned To: _____

Borrower's Phone #: _____   Date Item Is To Be Returned: _____

Item: _____   Loaned To: _____

Borrower's Phone #: _____   Date Item Is To Be Returned: _____

Item: _____   Loaned To: _____

Borrower's Phone #: _____   Date Item Is To Be Returned: _____

Item: _____   Loaned To: _____

Borrower's Phone #: _____   Date Item Is To Be Returned: _____

Item: _____   Loaned To: _____

Borrower's Phone #: _____   Date Item Is To Be Returned: _____

Marital status may change because of marriage, divorce or death. Regardless of the cause, you will need to notify some people and make some changes. This checklist has been designed as a guide during this time of transition.

CHECKLIST

❑ Revise or have will drawn by an attorney.

❑ Change beneficiaries on Life Insurance policies.

❑ Change beneficiaries on Pension or Retirement plans.

❑ Change beneficiaries on Stocks and Bonds.

❑ Change Name of Insured on Homeowner's or Fire Insurance policy.

❑ Change Name of Insured on Car Insurance policy.

❑ Change or cancel credit cards.

❑ Change name on checking account.

❑ Change name on savings and investment accounts.

❑ Notify your company's payroll department of changes in names and addresses, as well as tax-exemption changes.

❑ Report name and any address changes to the Motor Vehicle Department, so that car registration and operator's license may be updated.

❑ File address change with the Post Office.

❑ Set a date to pay your bills each month, so that no interest or late charges will have to be paid.

❑ Change name on real estate deeds.

INCOMPETENCE, DISABILITY AND REMARRIAGE

We have included the issues of Incompetence, Disability and Remarriage to stimulate your thinking. The conclusions described under each issue are for illustration only. If you decide to tackle these issues, please document your conclusions in writing.

Incompetence and Disability

There is a possibility that due to incompetence or disability I (or we) may become unable to live together or to live alone without outside care. It is also possible that you will have to make difficult decisions concerning my (or our) care, including moving us out of our home or managing our financial affairs.

It is our prayer that the relationships we have with each other in our family will enable us to plan together for such decisions. Total disability can happen suddenly, forcing more immediate decisions. Although we feel you will make every effort to care for one or both of us, we realize that such care could put unreasonable stress on you and your marriage and family.

Under disability conditions, we believe that our three needs will be:

- Love, physical contact and comfort

- Food

- Cleanliness of body

You could hire someone to meet the last two of these needs. Our greatest desire would be to be loved by you and our grandchildren (if any), even when we may be most unlovable. Your words of love and physical contact would mean much to us.

Remarriage

We have discussed remarriage for the survivor when one of us dies. We know that we have complete freedom to marry anyone with one condition. The prospective person should meet the approval of our adult children and of our closest friends. A complete background investigation including a financial statement could be used in this process. The Lord will, of course, direct and give peace to all with the right brother or sister in Christ as a prospective spouse.

Most importantly, the surviving spouse should have God's peace about the prospective marriage partner. The remarriage decision is ultimately between the surviving spouse and the Lord.

M E M O   T O   M Y   F A M I L Y

To: _____

This book has been prepared to aid my loved ones following my death. I also plan to refer to this book concerning important matters during my lifetime.

Revision will be a continuous need, and I have planned to review it frequently.

Most people desire that their financial house be set in order. I have completed this notebook as a token of love for my family. It will also help the professionals assisting survivors in the settlement of estate matters at my death.

Signed: _____   Date: _____